Manifest Into Reality

Acknowledgments
I would like to give thanks to the creator and everyone who helped make this possible.
I truly am grateful for all the support.
Thank you for helping this vision Manifest Into Reality.
Darlene - Edward - Sherman - Brandon - Nu'Rodney - Chinavia
BEP,DEP,EP,SJP,NTP,CTP,TLH,SND,STP,SJP,JAS,JAP,RLE,AVW
E,JD,AP,RLP,ADB,ACP,FNT,SDS

Contents

Contents

Contents

Contents

Contents

Manifest into Reality

It all started with a vision then the ideas came rolling.

I put a plan in motion a few more steps to take, I just have to stay focused.

With action I can't lose no matter how many times I fell.

There all lessons learned, I live in the moment and in the past I won't dwell.

If you knew or had a clue of what the future beholds,

Manifesting into Reality would be the key to the sole.

9

MANIFEST

INTO

REALITY

10

BELIEVE

Believe, succeed, you already have it!
Greatness upon greatness what more to imagine?
A life to live that is filled with passion.
A life to give filled with love and laughter.
The time is now to make a change.
Just believe in yourself and do away with the pain.
I am speaking real knowledge here get rid of all the fear.
Then Sacrifice what's needed take action
Make it clear, stay pushing to the top and even if you drop, it's only
temporary.
Start again where you stopped.
It's knowledge to be learned and you have learned a lesson.
See Practice makes perfect and believing is a blessing.

11

MANIFEST
INTO
REALITY

12

DREAMS

Dreams are those things you can't let go,
Manifest into reality and then you can grow.
All the hoping and the wishing will get you nowhere.
Its action taking; no debating it won't come out of air.
Put your mind to the test and have no regrets.
Focus hard on your dreams to bring out the best.
Put in work, long hours, plan and deal with the stress because every day a
new issue will put you to the test.
Have no worries, keep it moving. Everything will be good.
It's been a dream to live my dreams I always knew that I would.

MANIFEST
INTO
REALITY

14

THE FIGHT IN ME

I've got my back against the wall with no one in my corner.
If I slip and make the wrong move, I know I'm a goner.
My eyes open and I'm focused, but I still can't come up.
I just can't see no other way, it makes me want to give up.
It's the fight in me that's telling me I have to stay strong.
Although this pressure has me twisted I know my rights from my wrongs.
So if it comes to it, I will do my dirt and be gone, whatever the
consequences are I was made to be strong.
Just know I took some chances to live well and not wrong.
It took some time, but I have learned how to steer through the storms.

15

MANIFEST
INTO
REALITY

16

THANK YOU

Thanks for believing – believing in me.
Thanks for the blessings from a to z..
Thanks for the love that has been given to me.
Thanks for the vision, the vision to see.
Life is what you make it; it is a journey to be.
Thanks for the enlightenment and the wisdom indeed.
Everything is perfect with the right mind frame.
Giving thanks compliments the blessings, adds power and strength in the
saying.

MANIFEST
INTO
REALITY

18

THE WORLD IS YOURS

The world is yours. Anything you imagine is yours to have.
Flashy things exotic dreams no longer things of the past.
Everybody doing well, were finally free at last.
Through all sacrifice and struggling, I really learn that the rules you follow
aren't the laws to put us on the right path.
Open your mind, search to find the true wisdom of time.
And only then its true enlightenment.
No more blind leading the blind.
The world is yours.

MANIFEST
INTO
REALITY

20

TIME

Time, I won't waste it.
Procrastinate or forsake it.
It's a gift to have, and a gift to give so with all my might I choose to will.
The right to grow, progress, and live
Make the best of life, perfect my skills, enlighten myself,
Test the waters, dream big and keep it real.
The time is now, because when it's passed it's gone.
So respect the time, or lose the time.
Either way it goes, it's moving on.

MANIFEST
INTO
REALITY

22

THE KNOWING

The knowing keeps me going no doubts in my mind.
I'm focused on my goals though actions required.
Hard work ensures my dreams are coming to life.
My faith won't let me down I'm living the life.
I knew right from the start my dreams would come true.
Anything I could imagined I know I can do.
All my goals being achieved, it's no secret in life.
Through the knowing I have it all what I call a great life.

MANIFEST

INTO

REALITY

24

GROWTH

I started as a seed.
Now I'm developed and grown.
I was once taken care of, but now have a life of my own.
It took some time to get here, but I'm finally on track.
From the beginning to the end my life is based on facts.
The seed was planted and nourished, I'm grateful to be.
With time I'm getting better, what a sight to see.
Through growth I'm still developing and living the life.
One day in the future I'll know it all because I'm a part of the light.

MANIFEST

INTO

REALITY

26

SHOWTIME

The greatest production ever written was all about me.
My life story, my creation for the world to see.
My first scene into the world was a blessing to be.
Lights, camera, action.
Hey world are you ready for me?
I'm a star in the making, I was born this way.
Living my life and playing my part all day every day.
It's all skills I do with ease; I'm a professional at this.
It's Showtime why press rewind I have a life to enrich.

MANIFEST
INTO
REALITY

28

REMEMBER

I could remember how it was to once be a kid.
Not a worry in my mind the things that we did.
Creative ways, refreshing thoughts kept us youthful in life.
Taking chances when it's granted, not knowing our wrongs from our rights.
The times we had, oh so short, but great indeed.
I could remember every last blessing sent to me.
Although so long off in the past I often think back.
I can remember how it was that keeps me on track.

MANIFEST

INTO

REALITY

30

THE ENEMY WITHIN

Enemies come and go, but it's a process to this.
Some enemies you may not know, but they're surely content.
To bring you down and cause you pain is a part of their plan.
No one can really hurt you if you stay on your game.
Staying ten steps ahead can keep you on point.
So those enemies are irrelevant they'll never get what they want.
The true enemy at hand is the enemy within.
With all the doubts and the worries this enemy could win.
If you're lacking positivity it's time to rethink.
Put your mind on a level where everything can be happy, possible, and joy
are plain to see.
Those are some ways to defeat this enemy indeed.

MANIFEST

INTO

REALITY

FEARLESS

They say no pain, no gain.
A lesson to be learned.
Through all the fear it's clear with every step it's courage we earn.
No problems or worries, I defeat them quickly.
I'm balanced and focused my strength comes easy.
I'm ready for war no doubts in my mind.
My freedom is life though I'm not scared to die.
I made up my mind a long time ago.
I'll never be scared and I'll always think growth.

33

MANIFEST
INTO
REALITY

34

FAMILY

What true family is all about nothing could ever break.
No matter how hard times are, real family is there to stay.
What I mean by real are those genuine at heart.
Though looks can be deceiving it's wise to think smart.
In some cases you will never know until it's a little too late, and once the damage is done, it's done.
No time to pump on the brakes.
Think before you choose and consult your inner self.
See me I don't have that problem, my family speaks for itself.
There are very few to choose so I can count them on one hand.
And I'm truly grateful for them there's no need for demands.

MANIFEST

INTO

REALITY

36

MAMA

Dear mama we made it through the hard times to the greatest.
And we will keep on keeping on no doubts ifs or maybes.
From a seed up to a man, I was always a part of your plan.
And I thank God for the gift of you, and for all the pain I understand.
It made us strong, humble and wise, kept us grounded and opened our eyes.
No regrets to state, we live and learn, so in this thing called life we must try.
It's a blessing to be a son of yours you're a star in my eyes,
So, I thank you mama, no mistakes were made God blessed us with this life.

MANIFEST

INTO

REALITY

38

COUNT DOWN

In the beginning it's great no worries or stress and everything seems to be
new, exciting, and fresh.
If only we knew what we could do and what the future beholds,
Our lives would be grand and the story would unfold.
Time has told us all but we've failed to acknowledge that the past offers
guidance if we only would acknowledge it.
Don't let the time pass you by because the countdown is on. It's time to
take action there may not be a later on.

MANIFEST
INTO
REALITY

40

POSSIBLE

Anything is possible with the right mind frame.
Creating something out of nothing is a part of the plan.
When you vision on your dreams you can't let go.
Manifesting into reality is a sign of growth.
It's all profit to the soul. The prophecy is told.
Anything can be accomplished that's more than weight in gold.
So let the secrets all unfold the knowledge is told.
Every goal you set is possible, there's no doubt you can grow.

MANIFEST
INTO
REALITY

42

ONE STEP AT A TIME

I'm moving at a pace with no rushing or flexing.
I'm equipped with the knowledge and the skills I possess them.
Step by step I move in rhythm, no mistakes to be made.
With every step I'm gaining ground and with time I'll gain age.
The age of wisdom, knowledge, and power can be yours to control.
Just remember one step at a time – you can do this by staying focused on steady
growth.

MANIFEST
INTO
REALITY

44

CAN'T STOP WON'T STOP

I can't stop. I won't stop. I'm fully powered up.
My spirits high I can hardly try and we all no it's not luck.
The future's bright. I can see it clear.
The vision is strong with no doubts or fear.
The time has come to make my mark.
The days are long and the nights are short.
I continue to strive no matter what.
I can't stop, I won't stop I'm moving on
No time to pause I won't get stuck,
Cause I can't stop. I won't stop.

45

MANIFEST
INTO
REALITY

MY OWN ECONOMY

An economy of my own is a lifelong dream.
What was a dream is now reality, it was bound to be.
With faith, endurance, hard work there was no other way for me.
I'm goal driven, meaning every goal I set, I had to achieve.
Many issues along the way kept me focused to see that every obstacle endured was
enlightenment for me.
Now I'm shot calling holding down the fort you see.
It's all real, the economy I made for me.

47

MANIFEST
INTO
REALITY

48

IN YOUR CIRCLE

Sometimes you will never know until it's a little too late.
Watch your surroundings and stay cautious. Be aware of the hate.
All it takes is one bad seed to corrupt the whole plan.
So know that infiltration can bring you down where you stand.
If you feel like you've been tagged then it's time to clean house.
Reevaluate your circle then take an alternate route.

49

MANIFEST
INTO
REALITY

50

DON'T JUST THINK IT, DO IT

A thought may be okay, but with action it could be great.
When you think it that's just the beginning it takes work to be great.
Ideas are just the initial step, there's a process to this.
When building a dream it's good to think, research, and plan,
Then put your hands in the mix.
If you think it I suggest do it and when you make it that's great,
if you fail that's OK because the lesson learned alone will make you a
winner one day.

MANIFEST
INTO
REALITY

52

WHEN NATURE CALLS

We are all born with a talent,
The talent of greatness.
So many don't execute their talent
so the talent has faded.
Look deep within and it can be regained if you give it some time
with dedication, thought, and action leaving all the doubt behind.
When nature calls never resist, it's a gift to be.
Open your eyes go deep within and it's greatness you will see.

MANIFEST
INTO
REALITY

54

The Truth

No truth all deceit from the beginning of time.
Nothing but lies how could the mind stay focus and thrive.
We're all victims of our ignorance, so now the question is why,
we live in ignorance and feed the mind with false knowledge and false wisdom
throughout time.
The story has yet to unfold, but the truth will get told,
and faith can enlighten the spirit, heart, mind, and soul.
Only if you listen will you grow to gain the truth from within,
and know that faith that is guided can unleash the truth from within.

55

MANIFEST
INTO
REALITY

56

TAKING A STAND

At some point and time in your life you have to
Stand up,
When enough is enough and you are tired of the demands.
Sit yourself down and clear your mind.
Now ask yourself: the question "who am I?"
Choose your battles carefully and take no prisoners.
Stand for a purpose and hold your position.
Never back-down, Stay in it to win it
You have to take a stand your life is pending.

57

MANIFEST
INTO
REALITY

MADEA

For the one and only madea no other could compare.
The greatest granny that ever lived, who says life is not fair?
For many years she walked this earth,
eighty seven to be exact.
Through the hardship, sacrifice, and struggling she kept it on track.
A straight worker to the heart she just couldn't keep still,
and every chance that she got she used the power of will.
The power to cook and clean was a blessing to her.
She loved to do those things so it was also a blessing to us.
I thank you for the time that you shared with us all,
The knowledge and the wisdom I value it all.

MANIFEST
INTO
REALITY

60

FOCUS

Even when you're down, even when you're out, you have to stay focused avoiding all doubts.

No time for the shame, no time for the anger. Stay focused on your goals accepting all dangers.

See Challenge is a lesson and this is what I know and if you don't get challenge, well see you can't grow.

Time is of essence we need to move fast, accepting all mistakes and learning from the past.

Being focused is the key to reaching all your goals.

And if you don't believe in me, then avoid what I've spoken.

MANIFEST
INTO
REALITY

62

POWER

Mind over matter, no time to waste.
I'm trying to make it to a point, I can't even wait.
I'm so anxious so ready for this life to get better.
All my dreams and my wishes finally coming together.
Goals set, I'm on point, I have no time to waste.
I'm focused plus I'm making moves twenty six hours a day,
And if you feel me just believe me I get it all from grace.
I'm powered up from a source on this lifelong race.
See over the years I never knew that this was all adding up.
I got a sign from within saying be strong and never give up.

MANIFEST
INTO
REALITY

64

BLESSINGS

Every second of the day there's a blessing created.
The first blessing, given to us was life in the making.
Every sense then, we've been getting them, and I'm happy
To take them.
Why make a wish when I can create a blessing a
Wish is like guessing.
Won't count on luck I don't need it I can make
my own.
A billion blessings in my lifetime and I'm still
Going strong.

MANIFEST
INTO
REALITY

ACTION

It's time to take action, enrich-en your life,
with work indeed you can succeed it's our good given right.
With all the power we possess we can turn the dark into light.
With action taking it's no maybe this is how we live life.
learning from our past mistakes is one more lesson in life,
It may seem hard, but it's really not figuring our wrongs from our rights.
With action taking you can make it, it was written in life.
That those who believe will succeed, were all a part of the light.

67

MANIFEST
INTO
REALITY

68

SIN

Is sin what we really think? In some cases it may be.
Sin also means to deny yourself of your rights and your goals.
It's a sin to not take care of yourself and have the
Things that you want.
It's a sin to live in hate, negativity, greed and
to hurt others for the things that you want.
Sin can be considered many things, but keep this in
Mind,
Do what's right from the heart,
and you will sin at no time.

MANIFEST
INTO
REALITY

MAGIC

Real magic,
Imagine the things we create.
Pure passion, gotta have it and motivation is what it takes.
A little time and some effort can produce amazing things.
If you can think it, then it's possible, it's always good to dream.
Stay focused and know that your vision will manifest.
Be patient, stay strong and know you gave your best.

71

MANIFEST
INTO
REALITY

72

Adjust

The world is moving at a rapped pace.
How can we adapt to the times?
Let's site and think pause all thoughts, focus then just clear the mind.
In life we tend to step off track not knowing our way,
With every action that we take it's creating our days.
How many times have you wondered not knowing your way?
Now keep in mind know matter how well planned its risk we take.
If you can change with the times, then the sky is the limit.
Not many are willing to adjust and stay focused on winning.
The path of success is never straight, I can say that easily,
but when adjusting through difficult time it makes the future a lot more easy.

MANIFEST
INTO
REALITY

74

FOLLOW THE SIGNS

Let it be known there are many guides to greatness.
Pay attention look and listen the world is yours for the taking.
Eyes open and we still can't see the wisdom at hand.
Too many times we've missed the signs, that's not a part of the plan.
The over all goal is to be enlightened and we still can't see.
Too many distractions in our lives take our powers that be.
CLEAR your mind stay focused and then you will see,
All the ways and the signs that are given to thee.

75

MANIFEST
INTO
REALITY

MASTAKES

Mistakes help us grow, but one mistake can cost you everything.
Before decisions get made why not think up a plan.
The goal is to succeed and to carry out all tasks.
You never can tell where faith will take you, but you surely can demand.
The right to grow and be prosperous are blessings handed down.
Never think for a minute mistakes won't happen then and now.
If it wasn't for mistakes there would be no success,
So minimize all the risk and continue to do your best.

MANIFEST
INTO
REALITY

78

Shine

Welcome to the light it's a great place to be.
When educated with facts it's so easy to see.
The vision gets clearer no doubts can be formed,
no worries or stress, no fear I'm to strong.
I'm destined to be, a star that grows, and shines bright,
Illuminated with wisdom, and guided by the light.

MANIFEST
INTO
REALITY

80

Use It Or Loose It

Many talents we have in this life time, but it's wise to choose one.
Develope, Perfect, Grow, and master the task then move on to the next.
No time for unsernty it has no place in winning, and knowing what you want
is the start of the begaining.
Work on your skills daily and never accept defeat.
You either use it or you loose it, because if you don't it will get buried six feet deep.

81

MANIFEST
INTO
REALITY

82

Wish

If you had one wish one desire now what would it be?
A world of greed, A world of need, or a world of peace.
Choose carefully or pay the cost there's no take backs in life.
Alot of times our wants are not needed giving our out look on life.
If I had one wish it would be eturnal, and focused on growth,
because in the end there's never an end this is knowldge we should know.

MANIFEST
INTO
REALITY

84

A NEW LIFE

A new life a new beginning every day we wake up.
Some change, Some stay the same,
Who can we blame for our luck?
No one to blame, it's all a choice
every day is a new life.
Why point the finger? When you can grow, develop, and live a good life.
See all the hype about the world shouldn't even matter to you.
However, you feel just know there's better day's waiting for you.
Gain control take the steps to make tomorrow your best.
So shall it be a new beginning you've been put to the test.

MANIFEST
INTO
REALITY

86

Victory

Victory is mine so shall it be.
Within my heart and my mind there's no defeet.
I'll go the max at all times my faith is deep.
When asked how deep, I tell them invision the sea.
I take small loses and know that its not the end.
I learn quickly from losing that's how you win.

Note To Readers

If you enjoyed the book be on the look out for Manifest Into Reality vol.2
coming soon.

In the mean time come an vist us at ManifestIntoReality.com,
our online portal where you can stay updated, contune to grow
and discover how to Manifest all your thoughts, dreams, and wishes
Into Reality.